giftwrapped

giftwrapped

Practical and inventive ideas
for all occasions and celebrations

JANE MEANS

PHOTOGRAPHY BY SIMON BROWN

For Keris

First published in the UK and USA in 2014 by
Jacqui Small LLP
an imprint of Aurum Press
74-77 White Lion Street
London N1 9PF

Publisher Jacqui Small
Senior Editor Claire Chandler
Managing Editor Lydia Halliday
Designer and Art Director Sarah Rock
Editor Joanna Copestick
Production Maeve Healy

All photographs are by Simon Brown apart from those on the following
pages, which are by Ingrid Rasmussen: 9, 32, 33, 48, 50, 51, 62, 63, 64,
65, 82, 83, 104, 105, 122, 123, 130, 132 and 133

ISBN: 978 1 909342 56 9

A catalogue record for this book is available from the British Library.

2016 2015 2014
10 9 8 7 6 5 4 3 2 1

Printed in China

Contents

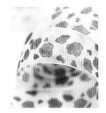

Introduction

I have always loved beautiful presentation, whether it is a shop window, dinner table, the way we dress or, in my case, a wrapped gift. My previous job as a florist also enabled me to experiment with paper, ribbons and tissue. I have a deep passion for my work, and love to be faced with a challenge.

As a professional giftwrapper you never know what gift you have to wrap next, and I love that sense of possibility every time I embark on a new project. Although I follow some core techniques, I treat every gift as an individual entity, thinking first of the recipient, and then trying to introduce a personal touch where possible.

My head is constantly buzzing with new ideas and I hope the pages ahead will bring some inspiration to your own giftwrapping projects. Thanks to the internet, I've been able to reach out to a worldwide audience, and I will never forget my first international giftwrapping client, Beverley, who flew in from Bermuda to do my course. I was flabbergasted!

Since then I have continued to run my own giftwrapping courses throughout the UK and have provided many private workshops, offering giftwrapping services and

tuition in homes and workplaces. I also work for many retailers and companies throughout Europe, with clients that include royalty, celebrities, couture houses and boutique stores.

In my job , no two days are ever the same. One day I can be advising a market traders' group on how to display hampers, then be en route to a TV studio to do some filming. The following day I may be in Paris, wrapping luxury gifts for royalty. In 2011, I launched my first DVD *The Art of Gift Wrapping*. It continues to sell well worldwide, and has been featured on national TV, radio and in the press.

My job as a professional giftwrapper and teacher was at first extremely seasonal, and I had little work for the first six months of each year. While advising retailers about their giftwrapping service a few years ago, I saw another gap in the market, for small rolls of fabric ribbon. Ten years ago I designed my first small collection of ribbons to test the market and today I have 100 bespoke designs, which sell online, at shows and via stockists that include Liberty and Fortnum & Mason. I continue to source lots of unusual trims and ribbons from around the world and I opened my first UK store in 2012, and continue to sell the brand through shows and pop up shops.

I've thoroughly enjoyed distilling all my giftwrapping knowledge into this book, and I hope it encourages you all to get creative!

Giftwrapping gives you a great opportunity to let your imagination run wild. With so many materials to choose from, it's easy to create a bespoke look for the recipient of any gift.

The Material World

You don't have to keep within the limits of wrapping paper either. Try introducing flexible wrapping such as netting, cellophane, tissue and fabric oddments. I also love to recycle remnants of wallpaper, vintage music script and decorative newspaper.
Decorations can be tied onto a gift with cord, string, raffia and strips of fabric, or you may choose from a huge selection of trimmings and ribbons. Throughout this book I will highlight the endless options available to you. By adding even the most mundane decoration to a gift, you can transform it into a creative masterpiece, at little expense.

Wrapping Papers

Although the art of wrapping has been around for centuries, especially in the Orient, it was not until the late nineteenth century that the upper-classes began giftwrapping in the UK, using first wallpaper then simple tissue. In the USA, commercial giftwrapping paper became available in 1917, and nowadays many countries produce their own signature papers, including Italy (marbled paper), Nepal (lokta), South America (bark papers) and Japan (washi papers), to name but a few.

I will never forget my first visit to a stationery store in New York. I was completely overwhelmed by the variety of specialist papers and, several hours later, I came away with a huge selection for my paper drawer that included Thai mulberry paper, Momi crinkle wrap, Egyptian papyrus paper and delicate Japanese origami papers. I absolutely adore textured and unusual papers and, when I travel, I love to discover what paper gems the local culture has to offer.

I also love recycling paper. The best types for reuse include old newspaper or wallpaper remnants, as well as vintage scripts or weathered music scores. It's so easy to trim off any tattered edges, and you can experiment by dipping old manuscripts or musical notation into tea to 'age' the paper even more. Once you begin collecting a stash of papers that are of different weights, textures and materials, you'll soon amass a fantastic collection,

ready for every occasion. It can become quite addictive, I can assure you!

PAPER WEIGHTS Commercial wrapping papers are made throughout the world and their weights are usually produced in the metric system as grams per square metre (gsm). A good paper to work with in giftwrapping is one that goes up to 80gsm (this is around the same weight as a lightweight copier paper). I prefer to work with papers that are quite thin but also durable, such as kraft paper. Papers over 80gsm (such as wallpaper) will not only be expensive but they may split easily. Using thick paper for small items will also tire your hands more easily. Tissue paper is pretty strong and its weight

is anything between 18 and 35gsm, which makes it relatively easy to work with.

COMMERCIAL PAPERS There are endless colours, designs and finishes of commercial giftwrap. Generally they are presented on a roll, in a sheet or as part of a flat pack. I often find there is usually less waste on a roll, and the holiday season is the perfect time to stock up, when there is a plentiful supply of rolls in all sorts of stores. If you choose a simple design such as dots or stripes, the wrapping paper can be used throughout the year for a variety of occasions. Many designers now produce reversible paper and some companies will print a grid on the reverse, to assist with cutting.

HANDMADE PAPER I love these papers as they unique. They are often mixed with fibres, rags, wood chippings, grass, leaves and pressed flowers (particularly paper such as Thai saa or mulberry paper). I have fond memories of touring India with my mother and seeing the hand-printed papers drying out in the sun. Each of them was utterly distinctive, gorgeous and, of course, lovingly created by hand.

BELOW Whenever I travel, I love to pick up interesting giftwrap in different colours, weights and textures. It's a good idea to start a collection that spans a rainbow of colours so you're prepared for every giftwrapping occasion.

Flexible Wrappings

When choosing a paper, it's a good idea to look first at the shape of the object you are going to wrap. If you are tackling an awkward shape, it will really help to choose a flexible wrapping. Many suitable wrapping materials you may find you already have to hand at home. These include netting, fabric, papers with a plastic coating, cellulose wrap, fibre paper, crepe paper and tissue. You could also try cellophane bags, paper tablecloths, silk scarves, napkins or recycled paper bags.

When wrapping gifts that are awkward in shape, are made from delicate materials or are items that need keeping upright – such as plants, bottles, china or works of art, for instance – it's best to avoid pure paper and opt for flexible wrappings instead. It makes the process much easier. I particularly love to work with cellulose wrap, netting or cellophane for horticultural gifts, while fabric scarves or silk remnants are a Japanese-style favourite. For those on a budget, source party accessories such as tablecloths and napkins from thrift stores. They come in a huge range of colours and designs, and make excellent wrapping solutions.

CELLOPHANE Originally made by a Swiss chemist in the 1900s, this is a clear film made from regenerated cellulose. It's flexible, waterproof and durable film which makes it an ideal medium to use for wrapping awkward shapes. Its waterproof nature means it is perfect for wrapping plants, flowers, hampers and display items (such as a prize in a fête or a festival or a competition, or as a gift set for a store display). You should be able to buy cellophane from your local florist or from a gardening store.

NETTING Often we associate netting with horticulture, mosquitoes and bridal veils. However, I love to incorporate it into my giftwrapping projects. A simple gift, wrapped in white tissue and netting looks fabulous, particularly if you have added rose petals, confetti or lavender seeds inbetween the two layers. You can find inexpensive netting in haberdashery stores or you could use recycled netting from old clothes or curtains.

FABRIC *Furoshiki* is an ancient Japanese tradition that uses a square of cloth to wrap or carry an item. It's a 'green' alternative to wrapping paper and shopping bags, and is also an excellent way of recycling old fabrics and remnants. Inexpensive silk scarves can be picked up from thrift stores and flea markets and make great flexible wrapping. The scarf can double up as an extra gift too, so make sure you know the recipient's favourite colour. Gifts for men may be wrapped in more rustic fabrics such as hessian, linen, cotton or hemp.

PAPER PARTY ACCESSORIES Paper tablecloths and party napkins make great wrapping materials.

Tablecloths are not only inexpensive, but are also available in jumbo-sized sheet,s are perfect for larger gifts such as luggage. They are ideal wrappings for plants and flowers too, as they are more durable than tissue when moisture is present.

OPPOSITE Celluose works very well when wrapping plants that are awkward in shape and need to be wrapped with a relatively waterproof material. Use ribbon trimming, string or raffia, both to gather the wrap around the gift and as a decorative finishing touch.

Ribbons and Trims

During the Middle Ages, textile merchants sold exotic ribbons made from silk and other expensive fabrics from the East, and they were worn at that time only by the nobles and the elite. Nowadays, a length of ribbon is regarded as an everyday item and is often used as a finishing touch in giftwrapping, to decorate clothes or hair, as a trimming on soft furnishings, or is worn as an awareness symbol.

My love for ribbon started as a child, when I would often collect lengths of ribbon from confectionery and wear them in my hair. I am now designing my own fabric ribbon collections, which are stocked in some of the world's mosst prestigious stores. For me, it's a dream come true.

I always encourage people to use a good-quality ribbon rather than a cheaper alternative, such as polypropylene or plastic ribbon. The finishing detail is the most important factor for any gift, so give preference to quality over quantity. There are many different types of ribbon, including woven-edged, wired and double-sided versions. Here are some of the more important types:

SATIN One of the most common ribbons is satin. Its sheeny texture comes in single or double-faced form, meaning the slippery sheen appears on one or both sides. I do favour the slightly more expensive double-faced satin. Its reversible design makes it easier to tie a bow, since both sides of the ribbon look the same. (See page 65).

GROSGRAIN This is a thicker woven ribbon with a narrow ribbed finish, usually made from nylon. The stiff ribbing of the ribbon can be a drawback when it is printed with an intricate design, or when tying a specific bow. This stiff ribbon is durable and travels well, so is a favourite choice for many mail-order companies and luxury stores. (See row 3 far right opposite.)

ORGANDIE Also known as organza or chiffon, this delicate ribbon is made from a thin translucent fibre, most usually nylon, and is an extremely popular choice for weddings and parties. I will often avoid this ribbon when using a patterned paper for giftwrapping, as it tends to get lost visually, against an overpowering background. (See number 1 on page 18.)

TAFFETA Usually made from silk or polyester, this is a lightweight ribbon that is often wired for additional strength. With its crisp smooth finish, it is considered to be a luxury fabric and was used for Princess Diana's wedding dress in 1981. It does crease easily. (See the ombré taffeta on the top left opposite.)

RICRAC This is a flat braid woven in zigzag form and is used mainly as a trimming for curtains and clothing.

Although it is tricky to tie a bow with it, it makes a great trimming or edging in giftwrapping and other craft projects. (See row 2 middle opposite.)

OMBRÉ The word 'ombré' is derived from the French *ombrer*, which means to shade. These ribbons have different gradients of colour (similar to dip-dyed techniques), or have hues that shade into one another. (See the ombré taffeta on the top left opposite.)

TRIMS AND TAPES I use many other trims, but my favourites include pom-poms, raffia, string, wool, sinamay, twine, cord and upholstery trimmings, as well as decorative masking tape like washi, to embellish my gifts.

OPPOSITE Ribbons and trims are often the 'icing on the cake' of giftwrapping. Take some time to look at the huge range of options available and start to collect a 'bottom drawer' of your favourite colours and types, from satin and grosgrain to organdie and taffeta.

1.

2.

3.

4.

5.

6.

7.

8.

9.

10.

11.

12. **13.**

14.

15.

16.

17.

OPPOSITE Organdie and satin-edged ribbons (1 and 3) are great reversible ribbons to use for everyday wrapping; If you have time on your hands and are good with a sewing needle, why not add some embroidery (2) to a ribbon?; Raffia (4) and sinamay (6) are good natural materials for providing stiffness and texture on a ribbon; Multicoloured tassel trim (5) and velvet daisy trim (8) are loved by kids and adults alike; A petal-printed sheen ribbon (7) is a great choice for weddings; Yarn (9) makes a great alternative to ribbon and can soon be transformed into tassels and pom-poms.

THIS PAGE String (10) is ideal for adding to rustic male gifts and for decorating presents for garden lovers; Baby-blue lace (11) is perfect for delicate gifts and baby showers; Cotton herringbone ribbon (12) is so strong it may be used as apron string as well as ribbon; This botanical embroidered ribbon (13) is perfect for trimming clothes and lampshades as well as for giftwrapping; Pastel blue gingham check (14) looks brilliant in spring decorating projects; Washi tape (15) makes a great alternative to ribbon; Wired taffeta (16) is a sophisticated ribbon that brings out the fun in bow-making; Bakers' twine (17) is ideal for miniature projects.

Embellishments

I always believe that an embellishment is a detail, statement or story that makes a gift more interesting and eye-catching. You can personalize it to make the recipient feel valued, and usually, with little or no additional expense, the gift will look more luxurious and tailor-made.

Choosing embellishments for gifts is a great way to unleash your creativity. Always start by thinking about the recipient of the gift and consider what item or decorative embellishment they would appreciate. This may be something as simple as a button or a felt pom-pom in their favourite colour(s), or as thoughtful as an item you source personally that may evoke a special place or theme close to their heart.

Children, for example, always love colourful buttons, badges and pom-poms; women often really appreciate artificial flowers, gemstones, and decorative brooches; while men often respond well to items such as a bunch of twigs or wheat, some nuts and bolts, or a decorative rusty key on top of a brown paper package.

When you carry out your annual spring-clean at home, you will inevitably come across all sorts of bits and pieces that could be pressed into service as great embellishments for gifts. Just think of all the everyday items that get put in a drawer and forgotten about during any one year and how they can be recycled – everything from ribbons to decorations from floral arrangements. They can all be stored away in a tin for later. You can also source inexpensive items from flea markets, thrift stores and antiques centres.

1 **GO RUSTIC** Wicker decorations look fantastic on rustic gifts and are easy to source. Other items to consider would be sticks of barley or cinnamon, and pine cones.

2 **SAY IT WITH PAPER** Paper flowers are readily available from craft stores and suppliers of cake-decorating materials.

3 **MELT WITH FELT** Felt balls are really versatile decorations. Not only can they be scattered inside a gift box, but you can also glue them onto your paper or ribbon as a fun decoration.

4 **BE CHARMING** Recycle silver charms from discarded bracelets or festive crackers. Or alternatively source bespoke charms from wedding-favour suppliers.

5 **LOVE YOUR BUTTONS** Keep a good supply of assorted buttons in a tin as you can use them time and time again as great decorations. Glue them onto your ribbon or giftwrapping paper, or wire them onto a bow.

6 **SHINE BRIGHT WITH JEWELS** Broken jewellery, chandelier droplets and other gems can be added to ribbon with a glue gun, and look luxurious.

7 **GARLANDS GALORE** Cut a garland into lots of small segments, and you will have a really good stash of decorations to use.

8 **BADGE OF HONOUR** Accessorize your ribbons with pretty fabric badges that you either make yourself or source from craft stores.

9 **POM-POM MANIA** Yarn is cheap to buy, and these fluffy pom-poms are really easy to make and look great on children's presents.

OPPOSITE Embellishments come in myriad shapes, sizes and colours. Allow your creativity free rein on these finishing touches, and use anything from specially sourced bought decorations to discarded items found at home or recycled from previous gifts.

1.　2.　3.

4.　5.

7.　8.

6.　9.

1.

THIS PAGE Silver pomanders and charms look stunning tied onto gifts, but give them a polish so they shine bright (1); Feathers come in all colours, shapes and sizes, and are great fun for giftwrapping (2); Corsages and feather hat decorations make brilliant clip-on accessories for giftwrapping (3); Thread ribbon through broken jewellery, such as this mother-of-pearl necklace, to lend instant luxury to a gift (4).

OPPOSITE Luxurious brooches will immediately add sparkle plus an extra little gift for your recipient (5); Paper doilies are inexpensive and add a quirky twist (6); Wired beads from my floristry days can be moulded into various shapes and look dazzling when tied onto ribbon (7); Give summer gifts an eye-catching finish with fresh or artificial flowers (8).

2.

3.

4.

6.

8.

5.

7.

Moodboard
PASTELS

To me, pastels bring back happy, comforting memories of my childhood – blancmange and candy floss at country fairs and children's tea parties with endless sweets and treats.

Other pastel inspiration comes from thoughts of playing in my grandmother's rose garden on lazy summer days surrounded by lavender, butterflies and wildflowers, or falling into bed, cosy and secure under a vintage fabric eiderdown.

Strings of pastel bunting on school sports days endure in my memory, as does the seaside from childhood summer holidays: pastel-coloured beach huts; sticks of rock; the ice-cream van; and weathered deckchairs and windbreaks. Much of the pastel inspiration for my ribbon collection comes from flowers, the countryside and food: a delicate pink inspired by peonies and cherry blossom; the subtle greens of barley crops from the family farm of my youth; not forgetting homemade lemonade and pistachio macaroons encountered in Paris.

A pastel palette is particularly suited to weddings and women. Despite their delicate hues, pastels create a powerful look and are extremely popular globally. I personally find them very comforting.

OPPOSITE Experiment with paper doilies, pastel cake cups and soft pretty colours in your giftwrapping.

Moodboard
VIBRANTS

When I'm travelling, the things that really attract my attention are the different cultures, textures and vibrant colours.

From the deep sunsets in Africa to the turquoise seas of Tahiti; the spice markets of Turkey to bright saris blowing in the wind in India. If there is one country in the world that inspires me with colour, it's India. Here, there is even a festival of colour called Holi Day, as well as Diwali, which is a rich celebration of light. And when I walk through spice markets, I'm inspired immediately and begin to dream up new combinations of vivid colours for forthcoming designs.

I also love the vibrancy of Las Vegas, where neon lights burst into empty streets and swamp the casinos. And then there are the bright lights of Times Square, New York, or Hong Kong by night.

Apart from travel, inspiration for vibrant colours in my ribbon collections also comes from fruits such as lime, kiwi and cherries; children's comics; flower markets; and fairgrounds.

Introducing vibrant colours into your giftwrapping gives you an immediate lift. Seek out the brightest colours of paper, ribbons, trimmings, buttons, feathers and tissue. They will each lend a striking statement to your gifts.

OPPOSITE Get the vibrant vibe with patterns in neon shades and bold colour combinations.

Moodboard
EARTH

The colours and textures of natural elements are always aesthetically pleasing. Think wicker, wood, soft suede, dried fruits and flowers, terracotta pots, feathers and lace. All of these are suited to any occasion or genre, and colours range from rich cocoa brown to spice-market orange.

The earth palette is often suited to gifts for men, and to me, brown is the undiscovered 'black' of the giftwrapping colour spectrum.

When decorating male-oriented gifts, I often tie spotted guinea-fowl or pheasant feathers together, then add a handful of sticks picked up from a country walk. Attach them to the gift with natural raffia or soft string and they'll blend in perfectly.

Brown paper makes a fantastic background canvas, and I'm such a huge fan that I designed my ribbon collection around it. It's inexpensive and versatile too; it can be stamped, crinkled or torn, and smaller sheets can be passed through your home-printer to create a personal message. This is one of my favourite looks, especially as it also encourages recycling, and it keeps costs down.

OPPOSITE There are so many earth hues and textures to choose from. If you thought an earth moodboard would be boring, just open your eyes to the natural elements and enjoy.

Moodboard
MONOCHROME

Monochrome is pure simplicity, yet effortlessly elegant in the way it combines black and white. To me it depicts Hollywood glamour. Think of all those flawless images of Audrey Hepburn and Marilyn Monroe, or of couture models reviving France's fashion industry during the postwar period.

As black-and-white as a piano keyboard; a chalkboard; the shining lights of a night sky; a chessboard; a retro television; a bride and groom; or a zebra skin. These are just a few of the classic monochrome combinations. Such simplicity is stunning in giftwrapping too. Two favourite designs in my own ribbon collection are one with black silhouettes and another with a sultry charcoal ribbon plus vibrant white stitching. It makes a real statement. Diamanté and silver give an extra lift to monochrome giftwrapping, so try some vibrant embellishments such as silver bells, glass droplets and pewter baubles to give gifts a real 'wow factor'. If you think giftwrapping in black is morbid, think again. Teamed with a white ribbon, it looks understated yet classic and elegant. It is the 'little black dress' of giftwrap.

OPPOSITE Monochrome doesn't have to stay within the constraints of black, grey scale and white. It may also be different shades of a single colour, so be inspired by a paint colour chart.

The best part about giving a gift to someone is seeing the look of anticipation and surprise on their face. Giftwrapping stems back to the late Victorian era, when giftgivers didn't want the rest of the world to see what they were giving to others, because it would show what they could (and couldn't) afford.

The Art of Wrapping

For me, giftwrapping always enhances the gift within and makes the recipient feel special. Even if you are giving a small inexpensive item, the thought and effort that go in to the wrapping are as important as the gift itself.

We spend a lot of time and money on our personal appearance, so why not on our giftwrapping too? In this chapter I'll guide you through the techniques and tricks for making your giftwrapping polished and professional. Even if your first attempt isn't perfect, a few practice runs should do the trick.

Wrap in Style
COUNTRY

Brown paper * Rustic * Country checks *
Nuts * Sticks * Dried flowers * Rosemary
* Barley * Leaves * Feathers * Birds *
Wheat * Moss * String * Botanicals * Rust
* Burnt orange * Wicker * Raffia * Pine
cones * Lace * Sisal * Cinnamon * Spices
* Wooden pegs * Beige * Weathered *
Suede * Leather * Gardens * Walks * Bees
* Butterflies * Rose gardens * Parched
earth * Sand * Copper * Terracotta *
Lavender * Bark * Gingham checks *
Wool * Sheep * Straw * Acorns * Ferns *
Rocks * Grass * Rusty nails * Pottery

Wrap in Style
RECYCLED

Old typewriters * Wax seals * Calligraphy * Rags * Ink * Stamps * Junk shops * Flea markets * Tickets * Old money * Antiques * Odd buttons * Piano scores * Rusty screws * Vintage cut glass * Maps * Blotting paper * Upholstery * Keepsakes * Trimmings * Old photographs * Rope * Crests * Shells * Cotton * Frayed fabrics * Wooden crates * Leather luggage * Library books * Denim * Industrial * Tweed * Coloured glass * Fair trade * Handmade * Newspaper * Cracked paint * Sewing machines * Wooden skis * Wire lampshades * Wooden toys * Enamel jugs

Wrap in Style
VINTAGE

Keepsakes * Birdcages * Victoriana * Lace * Bleached velvet * Paper straws * Shabby chic * Roses * Doilies * Candy * Blancmange * Comics * Storage jars * Balls of wool * Crochet * Knitting * Kitsch * Wooden pegs * Peonies * Talcum powder * Hydrangeas * Frills * Sewing patterns * Vogue * Classic cars * Bows * Cheesecake * Floral swimming caps * Silk gloves * Cruise liners * Postwar * Soda * Milk bottles * School memories * Rations * Retro * Posters * Movies * Romance * Vinyl * Housewives * Aprons * Afternoon tea * China * Silhouettes * Village fêtes * Neon lights * Voluptuous

Wrap in Style
GLAMOUR

Fur * Pearls * Tailored * A-line * Diamonds * Silk * Velvet * Corsages * Millinery * Feathers * Peacocks * Sparkle * Ruby * Marble * Flock * Brooches * Couture * Smoky * Fashion * Manners * Elite * Stately homes * Paintings * Sequins * Mysterious * Perfume * ArtDeco * Mirrors * Reflections * Sparkle * Lipstick * Yachts * Sun-kissed * Standard poodles * Chic * Air stewardesses * Candelabra * Deluxe * Lush * Luxury * Grand * Expensive * Chandeliers * Trompe l'oeil * Emerald * Gold * Bronze * Regal * Celebrations * Vibrant * Capes * Powder blue * Theatre * Dressing tables * Riviera

SIMPLE BOXES

For many people, popping a gift into a box is a favourite wrapping option, and I often hear this view expressed when I am tackling awkward shapes on my giftwrapping courses. The key to getting things right is to measure your paper at the start, otherwise you will struggle if you have too much excess paper to deal with – and we have all been there, struggling with bulky sides when wrapping a box. In our lifetime we will wrap hundreds (in my case thousands) of boxes but, if you follow a few basic steps, the finished items can look professional and the process be made quick and easy.

Wrapping a Simple Box

There's not a right or a wrong paper to wrap a box, but I tend to avoid papers with plastic, including cellophane (hard to crease), stripes (hard to match up) and flexible papers such as crepe. If you are using a thick paper such as wallpaper, it will help if you crease the edges as you go along.

YOU WILL NEED
Box
Paper
Scissors
Double-sided tape
Paper ribbon

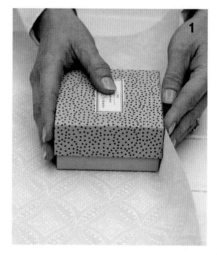

1 Measure your paper by wrapping enough paper around the gift, plus a maximum overlap of around 5cm/2in. Any excess should be cut off or folded in on itself. The side edge of the paper should be no higher than the height of the box.

2 Fold the paper under at one end by approximately 1cm/½in. If using double-sided wrapping paper, ensure you have your preferred pattern on the outside edge. Add a strip of double-sided tape along the top edge of the paper.

3 Bring the other edge of the paper over and around the box and then stick the thicker edge to it, so that the seam is disguised.

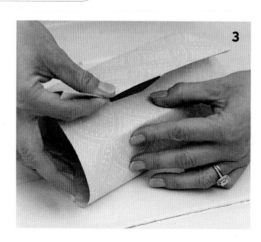

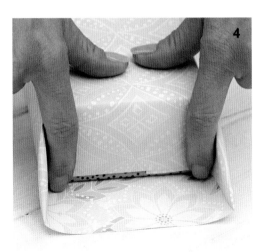

4 Fold in the sides and tuck in place with your index fingers.

5 Fold in the flat edges to form a firm envelope shape and a 'tail'.

5

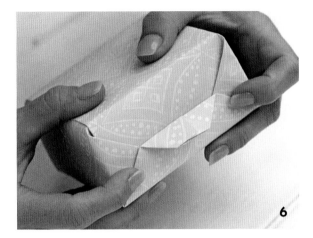

6

6 To get polished sides matching at both ends, fold the paper out half way, then fold inwards. Add double-sided tape along the edge.

7

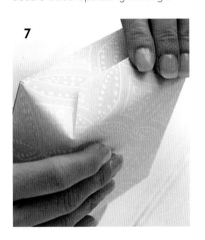

7 Fold the taped excess edge in on itself to form a neat 'tail', then stick to the end of the box to form a neat finish. Finally, add your chosen ribbon or decoration.

Roof-Style Box

This form of wrapping is a combination of wrapping a box (see page 44) and making a gift bag (see page 76). You form a box shape at only one end (for the flat end or base of the box) and the roof is tackled by squeezing the sides then folding over the open end, like a gift bag. You will need extra paper at the sides to achieve this. If you are adding some weight inside the bag, it's a good idea to tie ribbon around the whole gift bag to give it extra support. Alternatively punch a hole at the top, add a small amount of ribbon and finish with a simple bow.

YOU WILL NEED

Box
Paper
Scissors
Double-sided tape
Ribbon

1 Measure your paper by ensuring that you have a small overlap. Allow approximately 7.5cm/3in either side of the box, plus 2.5cm/1in at the top and the bottom to allow you to create the top fold-over and box-shaped bottom.

2 Position the excess paper underneath the gift so the seam is hidden (see Wrapping a Simple Box, page 44).

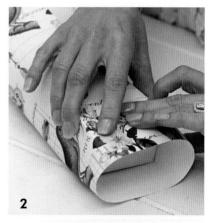

3 Remove the box from the paper and make creased folds on the four vertical edges.

4 The creased folds will form the box shape.

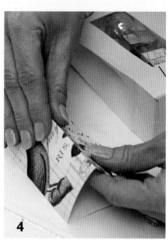

5 Place the gift back in the box shape and bring over the overlapping paper.

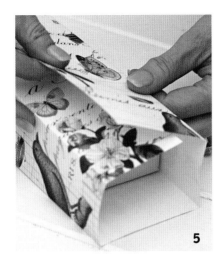

6 Stick down the overlapping paper with double-sided tape, all the way along the edge.

7 Fold the paper around the base of the box as you would for a simple box (see page 45).

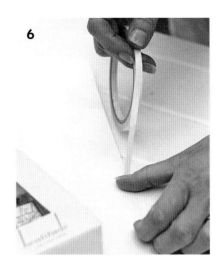

8 Pinch the two sides together so the edges form a crease (it will now start to resemble a gift bag).

9 Place the gift inside and fold the top over to conceal it. Finally, add your ribbon and any decoration.

Covering a Box with Japanese Pleats

I have long been a fan of Japanese giftwrapping and origami. During my regular trips to Japan in the early 1990s, I used to frequent a small chocolate shop in Ginza, downtown Tokyo. Here I spent hours watching the staff wrap boxes of chocolates in all shapes and sizes, and was mesmerized by their attention to detail. While there I learnt the art of Japanese pleating. Now you can, too.

YOU WILL NEED

Box
Paper
Scissors
Double-sided tape
Ribbon

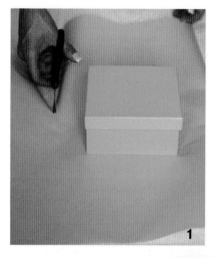

1 Cut the paper to the right size for your box (see page 44). Place the paper face-down in a portrait shape and fold it in half along the longest side.

2 Unfold the paper and place your finger and thumb on the fold a third of the way from the edge. Pinch the paper to make the first pleat, fold over 2.5cm/1in and crease it. Lift the paper up and tuck under to form the next pleat (to match the first one), and pinch, fold and crease as before.

3 Open the paper out and repeat the steps again until you have as many pleats as fit neatly across the box – stick with an odd number. I like three or five.

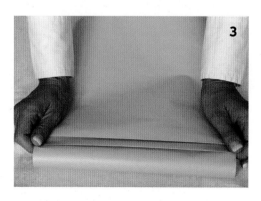

>> STEPS CONTINUED OVERLEAF

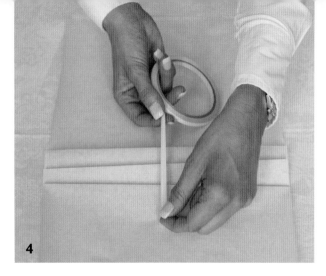

4 Turn the paper right-side down and tape the pleats in place.

5 Pick up the paper and lay it right side up on top of the box. When your pleats are straight and central then crease the edges (these are handy markers), and then turn the box and paper over.

6 Now, start wrapping the box, ensuring it hasn't shifted position on the pleats. Bring the long edge of the paper towards you and mark this paper with a crease where it lays over the edge of the box nearest you. Then fold over the paper on this crease and attach double-sided tape.

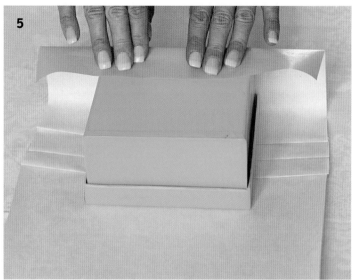

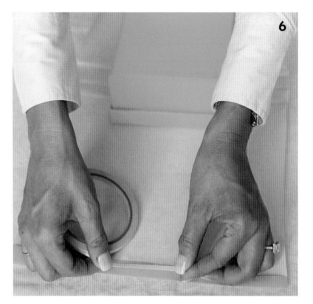

7 Bring the long edge of the paper over once more, peel off the tape's backing and stick down, so that the taped edge is neat and sits exactly on the edge of the box.

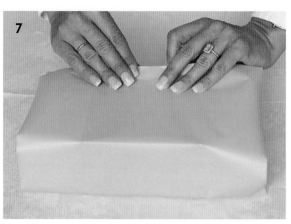

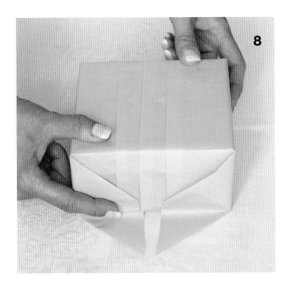

8 Now, do the sides. Flip the box over (pleats on top), push the top layer of paper down and push your fingers right into the corners, creasing the paper as you go along. Repeat on the other side.

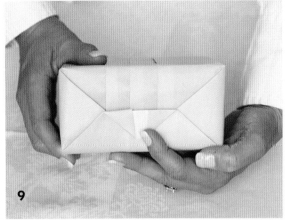

9 Take the outer folded paper into the middle, so that it's snug against the side of the box. If you don't get a perfect point, here's a little trick: take the flap and fold the paper back gently so that the fold sits halfway up the side of the box – you'll see its edges line up with those on the box.

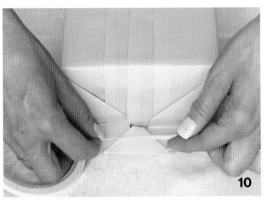

10 Cut some double-sided tape and stick the flap down.

11 Now, try out a few trimmings to decide whether you would like a coordinated or a contrasting ribbon.

12 Tie a simple bow (see page 84) and trim the ends of the ribbons at an angle.

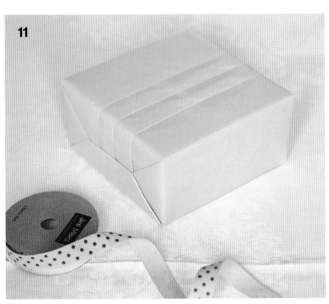

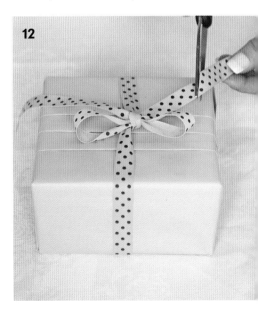

Double Pleating with Lace

I love pleated gifts that are wrapped in pretty reversible paper. This technique, however, looks good even though I've used single-sided paper with a plain white reverse. This style of pleating involves folding the paper over by a small amount at one end and pleating until it literally 'falls off the edge'!

YOU WILL NEED

Box of toiletries
Paper
Scissors
Lace ribbon
Double-sided tape
Pink ribbon
Fake rose embellishment

1 Measure the paper, and pleat the reverse side at the edge of the paper (see page 48). Then fold the pleated area over so it forms a decorative band on the correct side.

2 Add double-sided tape at the edge, then place some lace along the whole of the edge so it will be visible from the reverse side.

3 Add another strip of double-sided tape on top of the lace and stick down. It now looks like a pleated feature band.

4 Place the paper face down, pop the in the centre and bring the two sides up. Stick the pleated feature on top with double-sided tape. You can also add another strip of lace before doing this. Fold the sides as before and add your ribbon and rose.

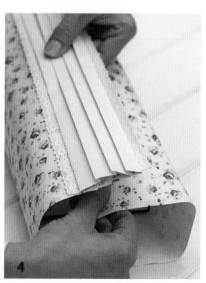

One Box Five Ways

With these few basic ideas, which each use exactly the same materials, you can let your creative thoughts run riot. Here I have used a reversible dotty paper to create five different styles that each make a bold visual statement. This is a technique that works really well when you want to create a pile of presents for a special occasion such as a birthday. Mix and match small and large prints in the same design for a dramatic effect. With the remnants of paper you can make circular decorations, pinwheels or a fan for a big statement (this is a great alternative to ribbon).

SIMPLE BOX WITH A HALF PINWHEEL

1 This is a simple and understated look with a half-moon pinwheel embellishment. Follow the instructions for Wrapping a Simple Box on page 44, and choose the larger spot design for the main wrapping. Make a half-moon pinwheel by pinching together the paper at regular intervals to form a fan shape. Attach the fan to the box using a thin strip of double-sided tape.

RECTANGULAR BOX WITH A SIMPLE CONTRASTING BAND

4 A simple box with a central band added on one side is perfect for giving a gift of shoes or a bottle. Wrap the box following the instructions on page 44, then cut a length of paper that is the length and depth of the gift. Turn under each end by about 2.5cm/1 in and secure within each V at either end of the gift using double-sided tape.

SIMPLE BOX TOPPED WITH A CIRCULAR DECORATION

2 Wrap a simple box as per the instructions on page 44, and use the smaller spot design for the main wrapping. Cut a strip of paper that is long enough at one end to create ever-decreasing circles within a circular frame at the centre of the gift. Attach one end of the strip to the end of the gift and tuck it in so you cannot see the end. Secure with double-sided tape. Next, roll the strip to form the circles and secure to the centre of the gift using double-sided tape.

SQUARE BOX WITH A BUTTONED PINWHEEL

3 A simple square-shaped wrapped box (see page 44) is graphically finished off with a delightful pinwheel that is really easy to make. Simply take a length of paper that is the same depth as the gift and pinch pleats at regular intervals to form a 180° angle. Repeat the procedure, then stick the two halves together using double-sided tape. Secure the paper wheel with double-sided tape, and use a sticky foam pad to stick a button onto the middle of the wheel.

JAPANESE PLEATING

5 Follow the instructions for Covering a Box with Japanese Pleats on page 48, but leave out the ribbon embellishment and present the gift as a simple pleated package. This form of giftwrapping is hugely popular in Japan, but deserves a wider audience as it is a really smart giftwrapping solution for all kinds of boxes.

Joining Paper

This style is perfect for wrapping a large gift for which a single sheet of paper is not large enough. Contrasting papers always look good together, or choose the same colour family or a mix of plain and patterned paper. This method is also a great way of using up your remnants of wrapping paper. The folded edge gives a really smart finish, and it looks equally stunning if ribbon is tied around the seam. The recipient will be so impressed they will never know about the paper shortage!

YOU WILL NEED

Box
Two sorts of paper
Scissors
Double-sided tape
Ribbon
Embellishment

1 Taking the top piece of paper, fold one of the edges under (long side) and add a thin strip of double-sided tape. Stick this on top of the other piece of paper (right sides out), making sure there is a slight overlap.

2 Place the box on top of the paper (wrong side up) and cut the paper to fit, allowing approximately 7.5cm/3in extra at each end and at the side.

3 Wrap the box as per the instructions for Wrapping a Simple Box (see page 44), making sure that the seam of the paper join is continuous in the centre.

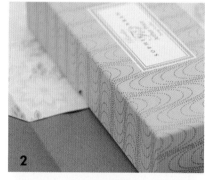

4 Make sure the ends of the box are finished off neatly in a simple V shape. Finish off by tying a simple bow (see page 84) and adding a faux flower embellishment.

Lining a Box with Tissue

There is something completely indulgent about a tissue-lined gift box that always reminds me of shopping at an expensive boutique. By adding only a few minor details to a basic box, you can create a luxurious gift at no great cost. Gift boxes are readily available, and I love them because they also make great storage boxes and can be reused many times.

YOU WILL NEED

Box
Gingham ribbon
Scissors
Tissue paper
Luggage label
Lace design punch

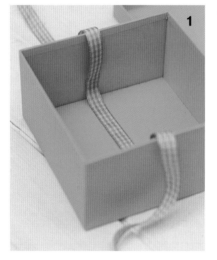

2 Keep your gift box to hand so you can fold the tissue to the correct width to fit the box. Lay the folded tissue over the ribbon.

1 To measure your ribbon, drape it into the box and allow a good length either side with which to tie a bow afterwards. Leave it in place.

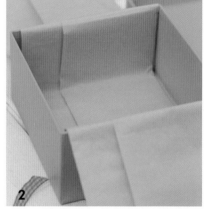

3 Add a layer of scrunched tissue to house your chosen object. Place the gift(s) inside and add any extra tissue for padding if required.

4 Fold the outer tissue layer inwards and turn one edge under to create a neat join. Secure the tissue by tying the ribbon around it in a simple bow (see page 84), looping in a luggage label name-tag that you've punched with a lace design. Instead of ribbon, you could use a sticker or double-sided tape to secure the tissue.

AWKWARD SHAPES

For many people, the thought of wrapping an awkward shape fills them with dread. However, there is a lot more flexibility when measuring material for an awkward-shaped wrapping compared to a box. When starting off this particular challenge, look at the shape of the gift before deciding on the wrap, as some papers will be easier than others to use in specific projects. You may even decide on a flexible wrapping, such as netting or cellophane, as an easier option. With a few embellishments tied with ribbon to finish, your bespoke masterpiece is bound to impress the recipient.

Wrapping a Circular Tin

I love to buy foodie gifts in the holiday season, and many come in tubes or tins, which some people avoid, as they're seen to be difficult to wrap. Let me dispel this myth and show you how simple it is. And whatever the occasion, you can personalize your gift with a bought or beautifully made embellishment to finish off in fabulous style.

YOU WILL NEED

Gift in a tin or tube
Paper
Scissors
Double-sided tape
Ribbon
Embellishment of your choice

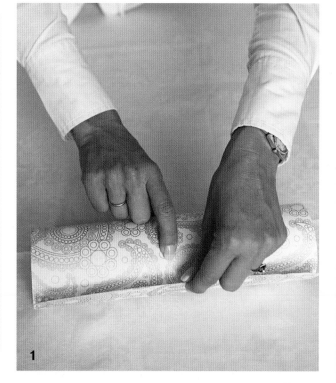

1

OPPOSITE I like to use patterned tissue paper to create a dramatic look, but plain kraft paper can work just as well and is a perfect foil for a festive centrepiece, as here. The white and gold paper is one of my favourite patterns. Here it's topped with a simple ribbon and some twigs of artificial mistletoe.

1 Measure your paper so there is enough to go around the tube with a small overlap. The sides should measure just above half way. Add double-sided tape to the long edge and secure.

>> STEPS CONTINUED OVERLEAF

'I accumulate suitably festive embellishments year round, not just ahead of the holiday season.'

2 To finish the ends of the tin/tube, make a series of pleats. Take the underneath layer of paper and fold so that its straight edge goes exactly across the centre of the tin.

3 Pull on the paper with your thumb and finger so that the next crease falls exactly across the centre of the tin tube a short distance around, and fold the crease.

4 Continue in this way and move around the outside of the tin/tube, repeating the creases and folds as you go. Don't push the tin/tube too hard as it could shift inside the paper.

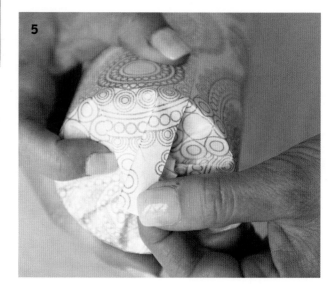

5 When you've got to the last crease, cut a short length of double-sided tape, ready to secrete underneath. But first read step 6 to check whether or not you need to trim first.

6 When you've finished the last crease, you may end up with what I call a remnant fan. If you do, simply trim it off and then locate the pre-cut tape and stick the last strip down. Repeat at the other end.

7 Take the ribbon up one side of the tin so that it hides the paper join and cut to length. Tie the ribbon and secure an embellishment if you like – I've used a bunch of artificial mistletoe. Complete the bow and trim the ribbon.

Champagne Bottle

Awkward shapes may prove a real challenge to many people. However, this style of wrapping is quick and easy. It is suitable for anything that stands upright, such as a bottle, a cake stand or a teddy bear. The key to getting it right is to use a flexible wrapping so you can give it some tension. I also believe it helps if you don't look too closely and do this project quickly, so you are more relaxed. As this bottle is heavy, I've used two types of tissue paper, strengthened with a layer of cellophane.

YOU WILL NEED

Ribbon
Scissors
Cellophane paper
Textured tissue paper
Striped tissue paper
Bottle
Twisted willow embellishment

1 Measure approx 40cm/15in of ribbon for creating a neat, generous bow at the neck of the bottle and keep to one side. Next, layer your three pieces of paper, placing the cellophane at the bottom, followed by the textured, then the striped tissue paper.

2 Place the two sheets of tissue face down on top of the cellophane in a landscape shape and stand the bottle in the centre of the paper. Working quite swiftly, use both hands to loosely bunch up all of the layers and gather a couple of folds halfway up the neck of the bottle. Using one hand, gradually make neat folds at regular intervals until half the bottle is wrapped.

3 When you get to 180°, swap hands and begin gathering the paper from the other direction.

>> STEPS CONTINUED OVERLEAF

4 Pull up the wrapping behind the bottle and hold it with one hand. With your spare hand, grab the folded edges into the neck of the bottle, giving it a slight pull, to forms neat pleats.

5 Continue pleating in the same way, using one hand to hold all the folds in place and the other for folding. Make sure the folds are evenly sized.

6 Continue around the bottle until all the paper is used up, making sure that you can see splashes of the striped paper at the top of the bottle.

7 Once the entire bottle is wrapped, bunch the folds together tightly halfway up the neck of the bottle and hold in place.

8 Keeping one hand securing the folds, use the other to gently tease out the folds into a slight fan shape for a more dramatic effect.

9 When you are happy with how the final shape is looking, tip the bottle slightly to one side to allow you to add your bow and embellishment.

10 Lay the bottle down gently and trim a piece of twisted willow to the length of the ruffle plus a little to tuck into the ribbon bow. Place this on top of your pre-cut ribbon.

11 Tie a simple bow (see page 84) to finish off.

Potted Plant

I often give plants as gifts. They are inexpensive, yet are also a very personal present. You can choose a rose with a name the same as that of your friend, buy potted herbs for a cookery lover or, as a housewarming gift, select plants that are suitable for the local soil type. If presented well, the wrapping may remain intact on the plant as decoration. I often see friends' poinsettias still in their wrapping, a year on! Use cellulose paper, fabric or cellophane for this as they are waterproof.

YOU WILL NEED

Potted plant
Cellulose paper
Scissors
A few skeins of wool

1 You will need enough square-shaped wrapping to cover the pot. Measure your wrap so it exceeds the height of the pot by half longer. (If the pot is 10cm/4in high, your wrapping will need to be 15cm/6in.) Bunch wrap around the base of the pot.

2 Gather the folds around the pot, just above its top edge, being careful not to cover up the flowers or foliage too much as you go.

3 When the whole of the pot is covered, carefully fan out the outer edges. Finish off by taking several skeins of wool and tie a simple bow (see page 84) around the pot.

Hand-Tied Bouquet

My love of giftwrapping started when I worked as a florist. I always believed that if you could wrap flowers, you could wrap anything. We often buy inexpensive flowers from markets, gas stations and supermarkets that look as though they need a little extra love in the presentation department. Even a simple sheet of brown paper can make your flowers look more luxurious. Here I have used parchment paper and tissue layers to make an attractive collar around a bouquet.

YOU WILL NEED

A sheet of tissue paper
A sheet of waxy baking parchment
Scissors
Flowers
Ribbon

1 Cut vibrant tissue paper and waxy baking parchment into four strips each approx 20cm/8in wide. With two mixed strips at a time, fold half way at a 90° angle so it resembles four V-shaped pieces of wrap.

2 Taking one large V-shape at a time, wrap the paper around the flower stems so the V sticks out at the top Overlap it with the next layer to form four Vs.

3 Gently gather all the layers, adjusting the V-shapes if necessary, and tie together with a simple bow (see page 84).

Vase

Vases make great gifts for wedding, birthday or house-warming celebrations, and here I've used a stunning Art Deco urn-style vase from one of my favourite interiors stores. Although you can use paper for this project, I prefer to use a flexible wrapping, and a remnant of your favourite fabric would work really well. Pick up fabric remnants from haberdashery markets or garage sales. Stiffen your fabric with starch spray to make it more rigid, if you like, and decorate with faux flowers.

YOU WILL NEED

Fabric remnant
Scissors
Ribbon
Faux flower decoration
Vase

1 Cut the fabric into a square shape, ensuring there is enough to cover the item. Fray the edges of the fabric by simply pulling away loose threads. Pre-cut your ribbon and flower decoration. Place the vase in the centre of the fabric, then gather the fabric around the vase, gently pulling the edges into the centre as you would when wrapping a bottle (see page 66).

2 When all the fabric is bunched together, use one hand to hold it in place and the other to wrap your ribbon around the vase. Then tie in your embellishment with a simple bow (see page 84).

Simple Bow

This classic little bow is great for gifts large or small, plus you use the bare minimum of ribbon. The question I'm always asked at events is: 'Can you show us how to tie the perfect bow?' It doesn't actually matter what technique you use to tie a shoelace or bow. The main thing is to imagine the layout as you are positioning your bow and take a pause at the end. If you're using a single-sided printed ribbon, you will need to make a few twists and turns on the way, so all the pattern is on show.

1 Estimate the amount of ribbon you need before cutting it off the roll. There needs to be enough to go around the box and also make a decent-sized bow.

2 Tie your ribbon around the box and ensure it is placed centrally. It is always best to visualize a large letter X to follow when tying a bow.

3 Instead of tying a knot, which will be hard for the recipient to undo, hold the centre of the ribbon tight with your finger.

4 Start tying your bow as you would a shoelace.

5 Before you pull the ribbon tight, take a pause and rearrange the ribbon so it resembles a perfect cross, with loops at the top and tails below.

6 Once you are happy with the positioning, pull the bow tight.

7 Cut the tail ends at a slight angle to avoid fraying, and to keep the ribbon within the boundary of the box so that it looks balanced.

Crossover Bow

This is the queen of all bows for a box. Immediately the eye is drawn to the polished perfection of the ribbon and the crossover of the bow underneath, which lies flat so the gift sits perfectly on a smooth surface. I find it easier if the roll of ribbon does the work (you'll be cutting your ribbon from the end of the spool) and you avoid turning the object upside down. This style of bow is well suited to large boxes but bear in mind that you use twice as much ribbon for a crossover bow than you use for a simple bow (see page 84).

1 Place the end of the ribbon in the centre of box and allow for a 15–30cm/6–12in length (depending on the size of bow).

2 With your other hand, take the roll around the box and bring it back to the centre so that the end and the roll are now crossing over.

3 Hold the end of the ribbon and the roll of ribbon firmly in both hands, as shown.

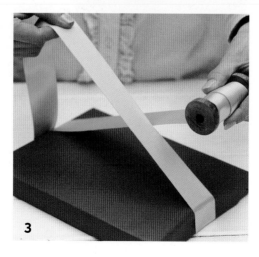

> > STEPS CONTINUED OVERLEAF

4 Rotate the hands so the ribbon is at right angles.

5 Once again take the roll underneath and bring it back to the top.

6 Use your short length of ribbon that you started with in step 1 as a measurement.

7 Cut the ribbon (off the roll) the same length as the shorter length.

8 Take the cut length over the top of the crossover junction and pull back towards you, underneath.

9 Pull the two ends together, centrally.

10 Tie the perfect bow (see Simple Bow on page 84).

Variation
CORNER ALTERNATIVE

You may wish to position your ribbon as an outer frame with a bow in the corner if you are trying to keep a printed logo or a design in the centre of the paper visible. It's also a good way of displaying a large gift tag and getting the balance right.

1 This time you will need to position your starting point near a corner and not in the centre of the box.

2 Follow the previous steps 1–9 and ensure that your bow sits within the limits of the box so it looks aesthetically balanced.

Corner Bow

Favoured by many chocolatiers and delicatessens, this is a perfect bow for highlighting the design of the wrapping or else the product inside (many chocolates or gift sets come with a translucent acetate lid). I do find it slightly more fiddly than other bows and it doesn't travel as well, but it is the most effective style for display boxes.

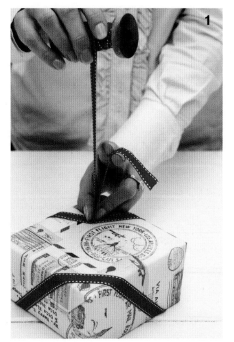

1 Do a rough calculation for how much ribbon you need, ensuring you have a decent length to make a bow, and cut the appropriate length.

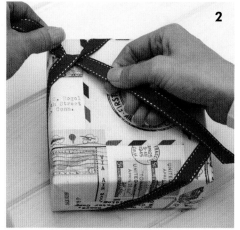

2 Place the centre of the ribbon across a corner on top of the box. The two loose ends now need to go underneath the box to the opposite corner, and be pulled back to the top again.

3 Tie the two ends and pull tight. Keep the tails of the bow within the boundary of the box, as per the simple bow (see page 84).

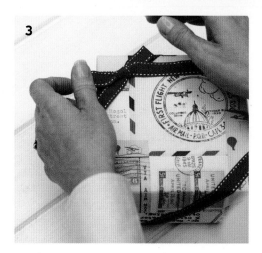

Spike Bow

This is a really striking bow that will add impact when in a bold colour. Always use a stiff or wire-edged ribbon to get the maximum effect. This is always a favourite with men and it's a fantastic method of using up old remnants and small roll ends of ribbon.

1 Tie your length of ribbon around the box, ensuring the ends are at least 15cm/6in long.

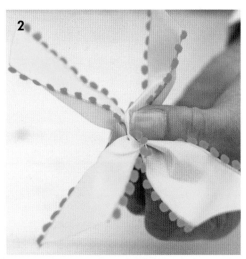

2 Cut additional pieces (approximately 6 will do) at sharp angles, each roughly 15cm/6in long. Pinch a couple of pieces together in the middle, splaying out the ends to form an X shape.

3 Layer the ribbon pieces at slight angles and hold them tight in the centre.

4 Now lower the lengths into the centre of the tied ribbon that is placed centrally on top of the box.

5 Tie the loose pieces in with the two ends (step 1). Arrange the ends neatly.

6 Splay out the ends of the ribbon pieces, and cut all the ends at sharp angles to form a spike bow.

Tailored Bow

This is one of my favourite styles and was dreamt up by accident when I was trying to make a replacement belt for a dress. You need very little ribbon for this project, yet the style is timeless and refined. You can also prepare these bows in advance, and they are an ideal finishing touch for any gift that needs to be posted, as it makes no difference if the ribbon has been flattened.

1 You will need to measure the ribbon around the box plus a loop approximately 15cm/6in long.

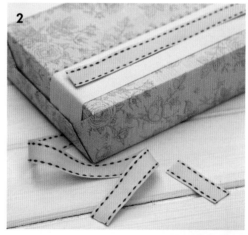

2 You will also need to cut a small additional piece of ribbon off the roll that will be placed in the centre of the bow. This small piece needs to be approximately three times the width of the ribbon (if your ribbon is 1cm/½ in wide, you'll need to cut a 3cm/1½in length).

3 You will need to add double-sided tape all of the way down the small piece of ribbon, plus a small tab of tape on one end of the long piece.

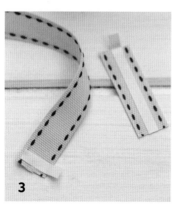

4 Form a number 9 with the long length of ribbon so the circle is 5cm/2in wide (if the ribbon resembles a teardrop, undo it and go in the opposite direction).

>> STEPS CONTINUED OVERLEAF

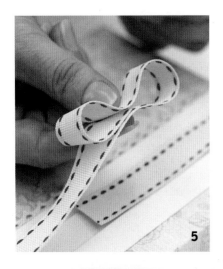

5 Squeeze the circle of ribbon made in step 4 as shown.

6 Add your small length of ribbon across the middle, ensuring that it is straight.

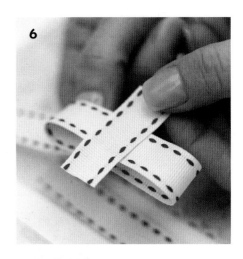

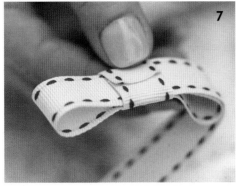

7 Stick the two sides together around the back and cut away any excess.

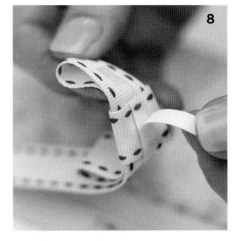

8 Add a small strip of double-sided tape across the back of the bow.

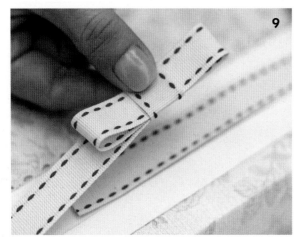

9 Place the length of ribbon around the box and stick the bow down on the top, ensuring that it is central.

Variation RUFFLE BOW

This style looks a lot more voluminous than its sister version, and it is much more aesthetically pleasing. You will need a longer length of ribbon to start with, bearing in mind you will need more ribbon for each additional loop. It is also vital that you keep the ribbon straight while you work on the bow.

1 Follow steps 1–4 of the tailored bow (see page 94).

2 Zigzag the long piece of ribbon from side to side so that additional loops start to appear.

3 Make sure the ribbon is straight, with the same number of loops each side, and then follow steps 6–9 (see opposite).

Bush Bow

This design calls for stiff ribbon and is easy to make. Its voluminous style is often seen on wreaths and bouquets of flowers, as decorations on large gifts, and also on wedding cars.

1 You will need to tie a length of ribbon around the box, wreath or bottle neck as shown. The ends need to be approximately 15cm/6in long (these will be used to tie the loops in).

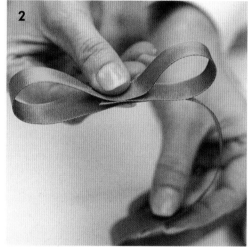

2 Take another good length or roll of ribbon and form a circle, then squeeze it in the centre so there are two loops.

3 Form lots of additional loops with one hand while holding the centre with the other hand.

4 As you start making the loops, pull the ribbon at slight right angles so you create more volume.

5 After you have made 6-9 loops, stop and cut the ribbon.

6 Tie in the collection of loops with the two ends from step 1.

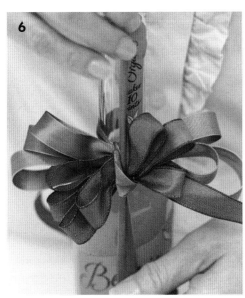

7 If you are using a wired ribbon, you can roll the two ends into circles, which will then blend into the loop design.

Labelling: 10 Styles

Vibrant gift tags (1); Type names or messages onto copy paper and make paper flowers (2); Decorative initials are perfect for personalized gifts (3); Slices of wood make great rustic tags (4); Type a name or a short poem onto copy paper as a decorative strip (5); Fresh leaves such as ivy are inexpensive (6); Laminate delicate leaves, and write a name on magic tape (7); Punch holes at both ends of a tag and add ribbon (8); Slate tags are smart (9); Pegs can be glued on as tag holders (10).

1.

2.

3.

4.

5.

6.

7.

Tom

8.

9.

10.

1 Vibrant gift tags make a cheerful addition to any gift

Vibrant colours really shout out and there's no better way to spruce up your labelling than with some fluorescent or brightly coloured gift tags. They can easily be handmade by cutting card and punching a hole. When wrapping a gift in a busy paper it's a good idea to choose a vibrant tag that really stands out. Children especially will love them.

2 TYPE NAMES OR MESSAGES ONTO COPY PAPER AND MAKE PAPER FLOWERS

If you really want to go that extra mile to impress someone, type out their name, a story or a poem and print it on copy paper. For larger sheets, head over to your local printer. The paper text can then be cut into scallop-shaped circles that make a really eye-catching flower label. Secure the layers with wire or glue. You also don't need to keep to white copy paper, choose other colours instead. Another great idea is to photocopy old photographs of your friends and family in order to create a personalized visual tag.

3 DECORATIVE INITIALS ARE PERFECT FOR PERSONALIZED GIFTS

I picked up these decorative letters while on holiday in New York, but you could easily make your own with some patterned card and a cutting mat. Adding initials of your friends and loved ones to their gifts will make them feel extra-special and save you writing a tag for them. The initials could also be threaded onto a tag and glued directly onto the giftwrapping paper.

4 Wooden twigs that double as rustic gift tags

If you have a saw and some sandpaper in your tool kit, head off on a country walk and pick up a good solid tree branch that would otherwise be used for firewood. By cutting thin slices of the wood and sanding them smooth, you can make ideal rustic gift tags. Great for male gifts too. Use them singly or group a few together.

5 TYPE A NAME OR A POEM ONTO PAPER AND ADD A DECORATIVE STRIP

To dress up and personalize a bland-looking present, you don't need to write a tag. Just write or print the person's name over and over on a strip of paper and add it around the gift with a pretty length of ribbon. It makes an eye-catching feature that is bound to impress the recipient.

6 FRESH LEAVES SUCH AS IVY MAKE INEXPENSIVE GIFT TAGS

Gardeners will love nothing more than some fresh ivy or rosemary tied onto their gift. Large, hardy leaves like ivy can be written on with a metallic gel pen. Their foliage will smell great, too, adding an extra sensory dimension and a horticultural feel to the gift.

8 Punch holes both ends of a gift card and attach with ribbon

Decorative postcards make great jumbo-sized labels. Simply punch a hole at both ends and thread your ribbon through to create a giant gift tag for a bold statement. For smaller sizes simply cut a square or oblong of decorative card, or you can grab a printable version from a craft website. Tags that are secured in this way always stand out, so make sure to embellish them in some way too. Stamp on motifs or messages, use calligraphy to write a beautifully personal name label or message, or use bright-coloured gel pens to get your message across.

7 Laminate delicate leaves then add a strip of magic tape on which to write a name

If you have a laminator, the world is your oyster. Here I laminated a mulberry leaf, added a strip of magic tape and wrote the name with a metallic marker pen. These are also fantastic when used as wedding place-name settings, and you can add rose petals, confetti and pressed daisies to name but a few. Delicate herbs and petals can also be concealed under a strip of clear sticky tape to make an eye-catching border.

9 SLATE TAGS ARE A GREAT CHOICE

Slate or mini-chalkboards make versatile gift tags. Simply write with chalk, and any mistakes can easily be rubbed out and re-written. They can be recycled again and again, so are a very 'green' option.

10 PEGS CAN BE GLUED STRAIGHT ONTO SOME WRAPPING FOR ATTACHING TAGS AND DECORATIONS

If you haven't got any ribbon to hand, simply glue a decorative peg straight onto the wrapping. I've decorated a wooden peg here with some fabric tape, but you could also use decorative washi tape, available from craft stores. The addition of a loose tag and some decoration would also make an eye-catching feature.

A beautifully wrapped gift can become a special celebration in itself – whether you are giving a small, token house-warming present or a spectacular piece of jewellery to mark a significant birthday. When wrapping for special occasions, try something unexpected that will make the recipient feel extra special. For children, tie candy canes onto festive gifts; for adults, add a single glitzy decoration. Even a decorative garland can be separated

Special Occasions

into many small components and used as individual embellishments. But keep it simple and use only one or two elements, as less is more. Or, for a silver anniversary gift at any time of the year, keep a stash of glass or silver baubles. When giving a wedding present, I always like to make a huge effort, as it will be such a special time in a person's life. Even a mundane gift voucher wrapped in tissue and netting with fresh flowers will look totally eye-catching. The idea is to enhance expectations and make a gift look so sumptuous that the receiver won't want to open it!

Festive

I love blending silver and white colours in my festive projects. Try using a glitzy, potentially overpowering metallic or glitter ribbon, then counterbalance it with simple white or pale silver paper to tone it down and add glamour to the overall effect. Partnering similar colours lends a rich elegance to gifts and is a style favoured by luxury brands.

White paper makes a great canvas for festive wrapping. However, it is often transparent and may mark easily, so I prefer to use a thick paper or one with a hint of colour, such as pearlescent or bleached silver.

Vintage jewellery, chandelier droplets and inexpensive accessories look fantastic when added to your gifts. Silver and diamanté complement each other well, and I've been known to add parts of discarded jewellery or interesting hair slides as decorations.

Items that aren't in this family of colour, such as pine cones, feathers and berries, can be transformed into a luxury embellishment by dusting them with a metallic or glitter spray (available from hardware and art stores). In this project I have also gone to the other end of the spectrum and added a metallic black box wrapped in a wallpaper remnant, embellished with a pewter wired ribbon, which would be suitable for a male.

If there is a particular time of the year when you want your gifts to stand out, it's got to be at Christmas. Festive gifts will be everywhere, with pretty packages in shops and vast collections of presents under the tree. This is your chance to focus on your inspiration and personality and embrace your wrapping with elegant colours and textures.

Many of us pick a theme or colour each year. The theme will often embrace the table setting, Christmas tree and door wreath, as well as the wrapped gifts.

OPPOSITE With so many festive gifts to wrap at once, I often go with a two-colour mix-and-match scheme, so if you run out of one colour, you have the other shade to use.

BELOW If you fall in love with an expensive sheet of wrap, use it to wrap small gifts and make it even more glamorous with sumptuous ribbon and fantastic jewel-like decorations.

LEFT Ribbon roses
can easily be made
by gathering your
favourite wired ribbon.
Wind it around a wire
stem and secure.

OPPOSITE Rich tones
and bold colours
make an eye-catching
statement, but really
come together when
you add a jewelled
embellishment or
sparkling decoration.

Gentlemen

For many, buying and wrapping gifts for boys and men is a challenge. I find that men love presents that have a personalized or special signature element to them.

To personalize a male gift, think of the recipient's hobbies and interests and try to bring these elements into the wrapping. If they are a music lover, you can easily pick up antique sheet music from a flea market and then attach an inexpensive bell from a child's toy or a holiday cracker. The recipient may love travel and have a passion for a particular country or culture. Old map books provide a plentiful supply of paper for wrapping, and if you want to go the extra mile, choose a ribbon that includes the colours of the national flag (as I have done here for Italy). Pastimes such as sports, classic cars and fishing are relatively easy to interpret, and even if you can't find a wrapping paper to highlight their hobbies, a simple embellishment like a golf peg or fishing fly will do the trick. If you do not know the male well, play safe and use classic stripes and checks in masculine colours for your wrapping, then add an understated wax seal for a very sophisticated finishing touch.

OPPOSITE Maps, classic sports cars and sheet music may all be used to denote special hobbies on gifts for men.

BELOW A classic wax seal or vintage tickets are a great way to finish off a male gift.

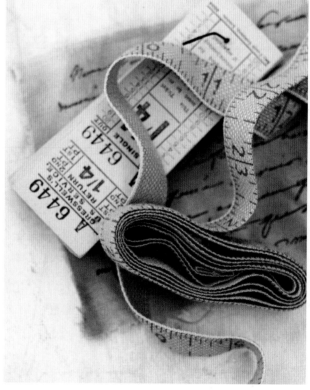

'Brown paper packages tied up with string' are one of my favourite giftwrap solutions. They are simple and inexpensive yet also scrupulously smart, and especially suitable when you are thinking about how to present gifts for men, who can be notoriously difficult to buy and wrap for.

This is where your ribbon and trimmings become very important, as they grab all the attention. For a man's birthday, try theming a group of gifts in brown paper and then varying the ribbons and trims in a colour-coordinated manner. Country walks are perfect for foraging and collecting sticks, feathers, foliage and fir cones to use as decorations. They suit any occasion or budget, and they offer a great way to be eco-friendly. Use the Earth Moodboard on page 28 for more ideas along this theme.

RIGHT Brown paper makes a great understated canvas and can be embellished with hand-writing or printed with a bespoke design. Its earthy tones give a warm appearance, and natural elements look great tied on as decorations.

Ladies

I love to bring in a touch of opulence for ladies' gifts. This may include tying in vintage brooches or jewels using a ribbon of luxury velvet for a spot of glamour. Hair trimmings and feathers look fantastic too, and can easily be picked up at flea markets and thrift stores.

You may also wish to lightly spritz your wrapping or ribbon with a fragrance or floral spray for an extra-feminine touch that will zap the senses. If you choose a delicate pastel look, tie in some fresh roses or peonies (flowers can be placed in a small test tube of water to keep them fresh), otherwise tie them in at the last minute so they don't wilt. Alternatively, you could add dried lavender or hydrangeas if you are hand-delivering the gift. You can also consider a rich and opulent look, or else style your gift to suit the personality of the recipient. If they are a keen gardener for instance, the country look will work better than other styles.

For special-occasion gifts for women, you can really go to town and spend some time selecting one of the many beautiful bespoke papers originating from Italy. These include delicate marbled papers and giftwrap designs that feature illustrations of vintage couture models. Or you can simply have fun choosing gorgeous velvet ribbons. Or create your own bespoke corsage arrangements to use as an embellishment on small gifts such as jewellery or cosmetics.

Keep a stash of faux flowers, delicate papers, gorgeous ribbons and special jewel-like decorations so you are always prepared for wrapping a feminine gift.

OPPOSITE Wrapping gifts for women allows you to work around the recipient's favourite glamour look or interests. Add a splash of perfume or room spray to the finished item.

BELOW Add embelllishments that have a feminine twist, such as faux flowers, rich velvet bows or bespoke corsages made from salvaged materials.

OPPOSITE Introduce
the favourite colours
of your recipient in
suitable decorations
for a personal touch.

RIGHT Luxurious
gift bags made from
thick paper look
stunning embellished
with jewellery (see
page 76).

Children

Wrapping for kids is often about vibrant colours, bold prints, texture and fun. Most children, of course, are more concerned with what is inside a gift, but making some extra effort will enhance their sense of anticipation – and impress their parents!

I think back to when I was a child and always opened the largest presents first. However, if there was one that was beautifully wrapped, I would leave it to the very end as it looked just too nice to open. As a child, I loved doing anything creative and would use up my leftover wrapping, gift cards and ribbons for making my own greetings cards with the contents of my craft supply box. Fun items such as balloons, straws and pom-poms will look great on top of presents, then add a wooden toy or a lollipop as an extra treat.

GO WILD ON WRAPPING

Stretch the limits of a colour palette and bring in fluorescent and neon. Make a statement with clashing colours and designs, and encourage bright florals, huge dots and eye-catching stripes. Let your imagination run wild.

BOYS WITH TOYS

Recycled comics make great wrapping paper for children. Many pages stuck together with double-sided tape will provide a large sheet for bigger gifts,

and a bold red or blue ribbon will finish them off nicely. You could also try an inexpensive decoration such as a plastic spider, bell or a wooden toy. For awkward shapes, try using some camouflage fabric.

OPPOSITE For children's gifts you can really go to town with vivid colours that make a real splash for a birthday party.

BELOW Match the trimmings to the personality of the child. Fun neon, retro comics or crafty pom-poms will all delight children in different ways.

THINK PINK

Most little girls love the colour pink, so you can also go to the other end of the scale and introduce soft pastels. Delicate partnerships like baby pink and cream work well, and a simple doily from the kitchen cupboard will make a great additional layer. You can loosely add it to the wrapping (with double-sided tape) and tie ribbon around to keep it in place.

PRESENTS GALORE

Little ones are extremely inquisitive when it comes to presents. For some the anticipation is too much and they will do anything to find their presents and open them on the quiet. To combat this issue, you could choose specific colours for each child for festive presents. After all, if faced with no tag they won't know which gifts are theirs!

OPPOSITE A bright pastel palette works very well on girls' gifts across a wide age range. For chidlren above the age of three, you could add an edible embellishment.

ABOVE RIGHT For a young teen receiving their first jewellery gift or a special book, try a more sophisticated finish.

RIGHT Everyone loves a fabulous blowsy bow, so combine pretty florals and polka dots with pleated paper for a fantastic girly statement.

THIS PAGE I really
wanted to go to town
with these thank-you
gifts for a boy's birthday
party. He loves red and,
of course, I couldn't
help but source some
soldiers too.

OPPOSITE Every child
loves a present that
looks too good – or
too edible – to open.
Place some fun items
on the top that can be
removed for additional
fun, such as candy or
drinking straws.

Romance

Romance is the pleasurable and expressive feeling that comes from an emotional attraction towards another person, associated with love. When you're giving a romantic gift, you want to emphasize the theme by expressing your love and desire.

Even a small, inexpensive gift can be transformed into a personal keepsake that will remind your loved one of you or make them smile.

WILD AT HEART

We often associate love with the colour red or crimson, rose petals and hearts. All of these elements can be added easily to your wrapping. Heart shapes are readily available on commercial gift wrap and gift tags, as well as chocolates, lavender cushions and even crockery. Less is more and you need to include only one element: it could be a heart dish filled with home-made biscuits, or a personalized hamper with your loved one's favourite foodie treats, finished off with heart confetti. Hearts may also be homemade by moulding wicker, ivy or wire.

DEEP DESIRES

The term 'romance' originates from the medieval ideal of chivalry, so indulge in rich crimson colours and tie in a contrasting vibrant purple ribbon. Sumptuous textures such as silk, taffeta and velvet enhance the senses, while flock and glitter paper look stunning. The paper I've chosen here (opposite) resembles an ornate stained-glass church window. You can also lightly spray the wrapping or ribbons with glitter or a favourite fragrance.

ROSES

I love fresh, scented roses in a bathroom or hallway. Dry the petals of fading roses on a rack to use later as decorations or scatter them between layers of translucent wrapping, such as tissue, netting or baking paper. Gifts can also be wrapped in scented drawer liners, or pretty floral wallpaper remnants adorned with lace and finished with a scent of potpourri oil.

OPPOSITE Small remnants of ribbon or washi tape can be added to token gifts to make them appear more luxurious.

THIS PAGE Capture the romantic element with hearts, flowers and pretty papers.

Wedding Favours and Gifts

Getting married is one of the biggest moments of one's life, and the occasion should be impressive, personal and aesthetically beautiful in every aspect. The custom of giving favours to wedding guests goes back centuries and is a way of saying 'thank you' to guests for helping to make the occasion special. Historically, five sugared almonds dressed in netting symbolized health, wealth, happiness, long life and fertility.

Nowadays, lots of consideration is given to wedding favours because guests will take home this gift as a reminder of the wedding. Favours can be traditional, ethnic or homemade; themed favours consist of anything from cakes and chocolate to trinkets and tree saplings. Often a favour will reflect the style of the wedding, and guests could expect to receive chocolates presented in small

RIGHT Giftwrapping for a wedding gift gives you a chance to get creative with sparkling, shiny and sumptuous materials. Silver and gold papers, netting, silk and satin ribbons and trimmings, and silver trinkets all work beautifully well.

LEFT Nondescript festive wrap can soon be reused for wedding projects. This box has been wrapped in mirrored silver paper and accessorized with a white ribbon. A silver pendant from an old necklace has then been tied on as a romantic embellishment.

OPPOSITE Add some lace or netting, or a child's toy butterfly, pieces of jewellery and other subtle decorations to enhance the look of a wedding gift.

terracotta pots or miniature seedling pots at a rustic-style wedding. A more glamorous wedding would probably involve small silver photo frames.

Equally, gifts to the bride and groom need to enhance the senses on their special day. Quite often we are ruled by a wedding list or requests for vouchers, and these can be wrapped elegantly with netting, tissue and romantic embellishments. Wrapping paper can be personalized by photocopying old photographs of the bride and groom, or by their favourite hymn or poem typed on copy paper or written in beautiful calligraphy. Pearl buttons, doilies, silver trinkets and other jewels create an eye-catching effect, and even if your gift

is small in value, this will make up for it visually. Also, owing to the large quantity and large value of gifts the newlyweds are likely to receive, I always suggest that you place your tag inside with the gift so that it doesn't fall off.

BESPOKE GIFT BAGS

Small gift bags can be bought commercially. However, you can easily turn your hand to make your own if you have the time. A pretty paper bag can be accessorized with doilies, ribbon and a miniature tag (see page 76).

CONFECTIONERY

Sweet treats can be presented in a whole manner of ways. Kebab sticks can be

inserted into soft chocolates to transform them into lollipops. Treats may also be presented in jars, bottles, cellophane bags, crackers, cones, envelopes, gift bags, tins or as individually wrapped items. By tying on a small decoration with ribbon, you will make the little favours shine, and the guests feel special.

OPPOSITE Sweet treats can be presented in a whole array of containers and packaging.

BELOW Make bespoke gift bags with pretty handmade paper or wallpaper.

'How do I love thee? Let me count the ways.'

The addition of a silk flower here brings everything together, colourwise and physically, as it's attached to the ribbon as it is tied. Match the flower to the bride's bouquet for fabulous wedding favours.

Simple paper cones with vintage lace edgings make for a stylish container of candy or other goodies to adorn a table or for a mid-event treat.

Baby Shower

A baby shower is a way to celebrate the pending or recent birth of a baby by presenting gifts to the mother at a party. Guests will bring along small baby gifts, including blankets, bottles, clothing and toys, and it is common to open the gifts during the party, so presentation is key.

Baby showers and other social events surrounding a birth are popular around the world, and they are commonly women-only social gatherings where a celebratory meal is followed by the giving of gifts for both mother-to-be and baby.

A GLOBAL TRADITION

In many parts of India, the expectant mother is decked in traditional attire with lots of flowers and garlands. In China, in ancient times, it was normal for the baby shower or *manyue* to be one month after the baby's birth.

In the USA and Europe, baby showers present an opportunity for the mother-to-be to turn up at a gathering of all her female friends and relatives (including the grandmothers-to-be), and to enjoy a celebration filled with anticipation for the impending birth. The holding of baby shower gifts is both a way of providing practical and useful gifts for baby as well as sharing indulgent gifts such as cosmetics, glamorous lotions and potions for the new mother, or heirloom items for the new baby.

OPPOSITE Soft woollen booties and cuddly bears always go down well at baby showers, and can be presented in pretty papers and soft trimmings.

BELOW As gifts are often opened during the baby shower, presentation is important on both the inside and the outside of the gift.

THIS PAGE Layer a pretty array of doilies and secure with ribbon for a spectacular display.

OPPOSITE A collection of small gifts can be presented in muffin cases inside a cake box for a really pretty effect.

House-warming

In my eyes, gifts for the home should be either useful or pleasing to the eye – and ideally both. A house-warming gift can be particularly welcome if it includes a basket of edible goodies that save you heading to the grocery store or searching endless packing boxes for something to eat during those first long, tiring days.

Plants and shrubs for the garden make another great house-warming gift and can be presented beautifully in a rustic trug tied with raffia. Or pick up wooden cutlery from catering stores or takeaway outlets: not only do they look good, but also you can also write names or messages on to the cutlery to transform it into a gift tag. And, of course, it doubles up as emergency eating utensils at a time when useful items tend to go missing. A basket of fruit or homemade cookies will go down equally well and can be presented in several ways. Try placing the goodies in a rigid box, a hamper basket, a plant pot or a storage tin, all of which can be reused at a later date.

One of my most popular blog posts ever was entitled 'How to Create the Perfect Hamper', so I know that preparing a hamper of foodie goodies for a new homeowner is bound to be a winner.

OPPOSITE A mini-hamper in a garden trug is a useful and beautiful house-warming gift.

BELOW Thoughtful finishing touches such as a length of thin gingham ribbon or wooden picnic cutlery elevate a house-warming gift to a beautiful object.

Tools and Equipment

I've always believed that if you're going to do a job, do it well. And this certainly applies to giftwrapping. For creative projects we can be resourceful and imaginative, but a basic tool kit will make all the difference. It's a good idea to stock up on ribbons and wrap so you have emergency supplies in your cupboard for that unexpected or last-minute present. Most of the common supplies you will probably already have at home, but other items available from office supply and craft stores will help complete your giftwrapping tool box.

If you are a craft addict like me, you will probably have a sewing machine, cutting mat, paints, decorative cutting scissors and punches hoarded away somewhere in your craft room. I used to be a florist and still use the rolls of wire, beads and corsage tape that I've had for many years. Try to keep your working area organized so you can find your tools easily. A small collection of crafty bits can be kept in a vanity case or storage box.

1 Gift tags are important. Not only will the recipient know who the sender is, but also the tag will give you a chance to write a personal greeting or poem. There are loads of alternatives, from fresh leaves to wood, so don't stick to the boundaries of card tags (see page 100).

2 Always opt for a high-quality ribbon in small quantities instead of smothering your gift with long lengths of cheap alternatives, as a ribbon is the finishing touch that is always noticed. The best way to store ribbon is on a spool or around a cardboard tube to stop the fabric creasing.

3 String and twines are a good alternative to ribbon, and can easily be made into pom-poms and tassel decorations too.

4 Chalk pens and metallic markers are really handy for writing on all sorts of mediums, from fresh ivy leaves to laminated gift tags. You can also use them to swirl designs or write poems in calligraphy on plain wrapping paper.

5 Craft, fuse and florist's wire offer a helping hand when making bows and ribbon roses. Choose a flexible wire, ideally on a roll, which you can find in hardware and gardening stores.

6 Scissors are key to good giftwrapping. They do not need to be expensive, but keep them sharp by cutting sandpaper or aluminium foil. Also designate a specific pair of scissors for fabric and ribbon cutting, as these need to be super-sharp at all times.

7 A jar of decorative beads and buttons will always be handy as they can become a centrepiece to a bow, or may be glued onto ribbon and wrapping for a fun effect.

8 Decorative masking tape and washi tape make a great border feature when used with ribbon. They are also a fun alternative to regular Scotch tape. Various sticky tapes are available, but the most important item in your giftwrapping kit is double-sided tape. Your gifts will look professional and polished with this staple item, and it's great for other tasks, including hem repairs and scrapbooking.

9 Pins are helpful for securing and storing ribbon, and it's always good to keep a stash of beads and pearls for extra decoration.

1.

2.

3.

4.

5.

6.

7.

8.

8.

9.

Stockists

JANE MEANS
www.janemeans.com
Ribbons, papers and giftwrapping
accessories

JANE MEANS BLOG
www.janemeansblog.com
Giftwrapping ideas and inspiration

**GENERAL GIFT
WRAPPING PAPERS**

CAROLINE GARDNER
www.carolinegardner.com
Contemporary stationery
pages 102, 103, 119

CAVALLINI
www.cavallini.com
Gift and stationery products
pages 11, 24, 25, 39, 46, 47, 92, 93,
112, 116

CHOCOLATE ENVELOPE
www.chocolateenvelope.co.uk
Eco-friendly giftwrap and cards
pages 1, 7, 125

CONRAN SHOP
www.conranshop.co.uk
Modern furniture and urban living
pages 61, 88, 106, 107

DOTS AND SPOTS
www.dotsandspots.co.uk
Cards and giftwrap
pages 12, 43, 55, 135

FINANCIAL TIMES
www.ft.com
UK and international business news
pages 10, 110 (used as giftwrap)

INKCO
www.inkco.com.au
Giftwrap and stationery
pages 4, 30, 104, 107, 120, 133

JOHN LEWIS
www.johnlewis.com
Stationery, cards and giftwrap
pages 3, 4, 71

LAGOM DESIGN
www.lagomdesign.co.uk
Giftwrap, cards and stationery
pages 51, 86, 87, 94, 95, 107

PAPERCHASE
www.paperchase.co.uk
Stationery, cards and giftwrap
pages 3, 7, 31, 84, 96, 97, 104, 105,
109, 120, 126, 130

ROGER LA BORDE
www.rogerlaborde.com
Giftwrap, cards and stationery
pages 3, 13, 35, 111, 115, 127

ROS SHIERS
www.ros-shiers.com
Wrap and stationery
pages 12, 30, 31, 103,

ROSSI (ITALIA)
www.rossi1931.it
Luxury Italian stationery
pages 11, 13, 40, 110, 111, 114, 116

SOPHIA VICTORIA JOY
www.sophiavictoriajoy.com
Giftwrap and personalized gifts
pages 26, 27, 103, 118, 119

SPECIALIST PAPERS

FOX AND LARK
www.foxandlark.co.uk
Stationery, fabrics and homeware
pages 12, 13, 18, 35, 42, 43, 44, 45, 56,
57, 60, 72

GLOBE ENTERPRISE
www.globeenterprise.co.uk
Handmade gift packaging
pages 5, 11, 12, 40, 43, 80, 108, 109,
117, 135

PAPER BEAGLE
www.notonthehighstreet.com
Giftwrap, stationery and gifts
pages 28, 29, 99, 112

PEARL
www.pearlpaint.com
Art and craft supplies
pages 11, 13, 30, 40, 105, 107, 109, 123

VIVID WRAP
www.vividwrap.com
Giftwrapping paper, bags and boxes
pages 13, 43, 61, 62, 63, 64, 65, 108,
109, 114, 115

CRAFT SUPPLIERS

HOBBYCRAFT
www.hobbycraft.co.uk
Art and craft supplies
pages 4, 18, 21, 26, 27, 30, 118, 119, 132

MARKS
www.washitape.co.uk
Japanese washi tape
pages 18, 30, 31, 111, 123, 123, 124, 141

PAPER SOURCE
www.paper-source.com
Paper, stationery and craft store
pages 13, 33, 48, 49, 50, 51, 104, 108,
115, 122

**STATIONERY AND
OFFICE SUPPLIES**

CASPARI
www.casparionline.com
Paper accessories
page 27

MOUNT STREET PRINTERS
www.mountstreetprinters.com
Luxury stationery
pages 111, 127, 129, 135

PAPYRUS
www.papyrusonline.com
Cards, giftwrap and stationery
pages 4, 5, 10, 13, 23, 25, 108, 109, 120

RAZZLE DAZZLE ROSE
www.razzledazzlerose.co.uk
Stationery and doilies
pages 23, 24, 25, 27, 127, 136

SCOTCHTAPE 3M
www.scotchbrand.com
Tapes and adhesives
page 73

WE LOVE TO CREATE
www.welovetocreate.co.uk
Homeware, accessories and gifts
pages 26, 27, 30, 31

WRITING MATERIALS

MANUSCRIPT PEN COMPANY
www.calligraphy.co.uk
Calligraphy pens and wax seals
pages 9, 36, 110, 111

PILOT PENS
www.pilotpen.co.uk
Pens and markers
page 130

SHARPIE PENS
www.sharpie.co.uk
Markers and pens
page 141

RIBBONS AND TRIMS

MAY ARTS
www.mayarts.com
Ribbons and trimmings
pages 1, 17, 24, 25, 30,1 25, 127

WOOL AND TWINE

TWOOL
www.twool.co.uk
British natural wool twine
pages 18, 70, 113

**DECORATIONS AND
EMBELLISHMENTS**

DOTCOMGIFTSHOP
www.dotcomgiftshop.com
Gifts and decorations
pages 4, 5, 7, 39, 52, 53, 120, 121, 122,
124, 131, 137

EAST OF INDIA
www.eastofindia.co.uk
Gifts and decorations
pages 21, 28, 29, 36, 103, 110, 111, 123,
125

ETSY
www.etsy.com
Handmade and vintage items
pages 137, 138

GIFTS AND ACCESSORIES

ADVENTINO
www.adventino.co.uk
Furnishings, accessories and gifts
page 125   .

AMICA
www.amicaaccessories.com
Felt bags and decorations
pages 21, 26, 27, 31, 118, 119

FABINDIA
www.fabindia.com
Ethnic furnishings and fabrics
pages 61, 117

ISETAN
www.isetan.com.sg
Clothing, homeware and stationery
pages 66, 67, 68, 69, 70

JENNY ARNOTT
www.jennyarnott.co.uk
Cards, gifts and badges
pages 5, 21, 24, 119, 137

MISS ETOILE
www.missetoile.dk
Home accessories and textiles
pages 24, 25, 123, 137

MYER
www.myer.com.au
Homeware, stationery and gifts
pages 15, 106, 108, 126, 134

NOT ON THE HIGH STREET
www.notonthehighstreet.com
Personalized and unique gifts
pages 21, 125, 137

PEDLARS
www.pedlars.co.uk
Vintage accessories and gadgets
pages 9, 11, 36, 88, 112, 115,
122, 126, 141

PETRA BOASE
www.petraboase.com
Stationery, decorations and bird clips
page 144

HOME AND INTERIORS

B+Q
www.diy.com
Homeware and DIY
pages 76, 77, 78, 79

DAVID JONES
www.davidjones.com.au
Clothing, homeware and stationery
pages 2, 24, 106, 126

DREAMWALLS
www.dreamwall.co.uk
Wall panels and décor
pages 55, 121, 127, 135

FOLLIE
www.follie.co.uk
Home accessories and gifts
pages 2, 7, 22, 23, 27, 40, 76,
77, 79, 84, 108, 117, 125

LAKELAND
www.lakeland.co.uk
Baking supplies and accessories
pages 4, 70, 121, 124, 130, 136, 137

LE BON MARCHE
www.lebonmarche.com
Home, fashion and haberdashery
pages 84, 135

LEONARDS INTERIORS
www.leonardsinteriors.co.uk
Scandinavian-style accessories and
interiors
pages 2, 72, 107, 126

PINS AND RIBBONS
www.pinsandribbons.co.uk
Soft furnishings and accessories
page 72

RALPH LAUREN
www.ralphlauren.com
Clothes, homeware and bedding
page 115

SOPHIE ALLPORT
www.sophieallport.com
China, textiles and stationery
pages 58, 59

SOPHIE CONRAN
www.sophieconran.com
Unique gifts and home accessories
pages 9, 19, 36, 44, 45, 56, 57,

TARGET
www.target.com
Home décor
pages 2, 4, 21, 104, 105, 120, 121,
123, 137

CLOTHES

JACK WILLS
www.jackwills.com
British clothing and accessories
pages 79, 80, 81

JAEGER
www.jaeger.co.uk
Luxury British clothing
pages 74, 75

UNITED ODD SOCKS
www.unitedoddsocks.com
Mismatched sock sets
page 119

CHILDREN AND BABY GIFTS

BUBS BEARS
www.bubsbears.com
Handmade keepsake bears
page 135

FLUFFY DUCKLING KNITS
www.fluffyducklingknits.co.uk
Hand-knitted baby items
pages 134, 135, 137

GAP
www.gap.com
Clothes for women, men, babies
and kids
page 137

BEAUTY AND FRAGRANCE

BEATITUDE
www.beatitudeproducts.co.uk
Face and body aromatherapy oils
pages 46, 47

HEYLAND AND WHITTLE
www.heylandandwhittle.co.uk
Soap and herbal merchants
pages 52, 53, 116

PENHALIGONS
www.penhaligons.com
Luxury gifts and fragrance
page 115

POLLYFIELDS
www.pollyfields.co.uk
Fragrant decorations and oils
pages 28, 29, 124, 125

FOOD AND DRINK

BELVOIR CORDIALS
www.belvoirfruitfarms.co.uk
Fruit cordials and presses
pages 100, 101

CARVED ANGEL
www.thecarvedangel.com
Luxury food and puddings
page 73

CHOC AMOR
www.chocamor.co.uk
Luxury chocolates
pages 73, 120, 125, 131

FORTNUM AND MASON
www.fortnumandmason.com
Fine foods, hampers, teas and wine
pages 62, 63, 64, 65, 73

LAURENT-PERRIER
www.laurent-perrier.com
Champagne
pages 66, 67, 68, 69

THE QUINCE TREE
www.thequincetree.com
Café, delicatessen and gifts
pages 73, 122, 125, 138, 139

GARDENING AND FLORISTRY

CLIFTON NURSERIES
www.clifton.co.uk
Garden centre and plant nursery
pages 15, 21, 27, 35, 52, 53, 63, 65, 70,
81, 112, 116, 125, 126, 127, 135, 138, 139

COUNTRY BASKETS
www.countrybaskets.co.uk
Artificial flowers and floristry supplies
pages 10, 11, 18, 21, 27, 32, 44, 72, 73,
132

FLOWERS BY SUZANNE
www.flowers-lincoln.co.uk
Wedding bouquets and floral creations
pages 66, 67, 68, 69, 71

MARK HOWE FLOWERS
www.markhoweflowers.com
Flowers, arrangements and interiors
pages 44, 113, 125

JEWELLERY AND MILLINERY

KANSHI JEWELLERY
www.kanshijewellery.co.uk
Bespoke jewellery
pages 40, 114

SAM SMITH AT BEAUTY BY KATE
www.woodhallspa.org
Button jewellery
page 120

STEPHANIE SHINE MILLINERY
www.weddingbinder.co.uk
Hats, feathers and hairpieces
pages 22, 29, 31, 40, 84, 109, 112, 115,
116, 131

Acknowledgments

For years it has been a dream to put all of my creative ideas in to my very own giftwrapping book.
I have been approached by publishers, but wanted to write my signature book, with a specific look and feel, oozing
with beautiful photography and simple steps. I approached one publisher only, one whose books I buy, read and
admire, and one who was highly recommended by other authors. It was Jacqui Small.

I would like to say a huge thank you to Jacqui Small and Jo Copestick, who believed in me, knowing that I was a
risky new author, and trusted me to deliver to a global audience. Despite the tight deadlines, it has been an absolute
delight working with Claire, Lydia, Maeve, Liz, Jessica, Sian, Ruth and the JS team behind the scenes.

I thoroughly enjoyed shoot days with bird-loving Sarah, Astrid and our photographer, Simon Brown.
Your styling and photography are incredible.

A huge thank you to Wendy and Matthew from Clifton Nurseries, who have been so generous and kind,
allowing us to shoot at their prestigious location, plus the team at the Quince Tree Café on site,
who fed us incredible lunches and cake.

I'm very grateful to the stockists and suppliers, who went out of their way sending loans and
giveaways and getting clearance, making this book possible.

Thank you to Kirstie Allsopp and Lisa, who continue to promote crafts, and all of the customers,
clients, bloggers, businesses and friends who have believed in me.

I knew the workload of being a company director, designer, teacher, presenter, blogger, wife and author, all at the
same time, would be challenging, and I appreciate the much-needed support and cups of tea from Caroline, Sarah,
Helen and my other staff, my parents, family and close friends.

Most of all, I would like to thank David. You have been an absolute rock.